Bake with Shapes

Kim Nguyen
Illustrated by Bob Masheris
Photographed by Bill Burlingham

Rigby • Steck-Vaughn

www.HarcourtAchieve.com
1.800.531.5015

Let's bake with shapes.

Here are the pans.

This pan looks like a circle.

circle

4

5

This pan looks
like a triangle.

triangle

This pan looks like a rectangle.

rectangle

This pan looks like a square.

square

This pan looks
like a star.

star

This pan looks
like a heart.

heart

We made cakes with ALL
the shapes!